ANCIENT CHINA

ANCIENT CIVILIZATIONS IN REVIEW

By Seth Lynch

Enslow Publishing

Please visit our website, www.enslow.com. For a free color catalog of all our high-quality books, call toll free 1-800-398-2504 or fax 1-877-980-4454.

Library of Congress Cataloging-in-Publication Data
Names: Lynch, Seth, author.
Title: Ancient China / Seth Lynch.
Description: Buffalo, New York : Enslow Publishing, [2025] | Series: Ancient civilizations in review | Includes index.
Identifiers: LCCN 2024020688 | ISBN 9781978542679 (library binding) | ISBN 9781978542662 (paperback) | ISBN 9781978542686 (ebook)
Subjects: LCSH: China–Civilization–To 221 B.C.–Juvenile literature. | China–Civilization–221 B.C.-960 A.D.–Juvenile literature.
Classification: LCC DS741.65 .L96 2025 | DDC 931–dc23/eng/20240503
LC record available at https://lccn.loc.gov/2024020688

Published in 2025 by
Enslow Publishing
2544 Clinton Street
Buffalo, NY 14224

Portions of this work were originally authored by Daniel R. Faust and published as *Ancient China.* All new material this edition authored by Seth Lynch.

Designer: Leslie Taylor
Editor: Kristen Nelson

Photo credits: Cover (great wall) Sophy Ru/Shutterstock, (dragon) Gilmanshin/Shutterstock.com, (back cover) Robert Way/Shutterstock.com; Cover and series art (vintage map) Andrey_Kuzmin/Shutterstock.com (brush strokes) ozzichka/Shutterstock.com, (font) MagicPics/Shutterstock.com; p. 5 Anson_shutterstock/Shutterstock.com; p. 7 Mo Wu/Shutterstock.com; p. 8 Sander Bos/Shutterstock.com; p. 9 Lerner Vadim/Shutterstock.com; p. 11 Ma Linl/File:King Yu of Xia.jpg_commons.wikimedia.org; p. 12 Claire H. from New York City, USA/File:Shang dynasty curved bronze knives with turquoise inlays and animal pommel. 12th-11th century BCE.jpg_commons.wikimedia.org; p. 13 National Palace Museum/File:Pan water vessel with coiling dragon pattern, Late Shang Dynasty (c.14th - Mid 11th Century B.C.E.).tif_commons.wikimedia.org; p. 15 Shan_shan/Shutterstock.com, (background lettering) Gsklee at English Wikipedia/File:XiaozhuanQinquan sized.jpg_commons.wikimedia.org; p. 17 Geermy/Shutterstock.com; p. 19 zhu difeng/Shutterstock.com; p. 20 cl2004lhy/Shutterstock.com; p. 21 jejim/Shutterstock.com; p. 23 drs2biz/File:Silk from Mawangdui.jpg_commons.wikimedia.org, (inset) anonymous Hunan Museum/File:Mawangdui painted silk funeral banner.jpg_commons.wikimedia.org; p. 24 Chris55/File:Paperbook+256.jpg_commons.wikimedia.org; p. 25 Rosemania/File:China qing blue.JPG_commons.wikimedia.org; p. 27 Araniko/File:YuanEmperorAlbumKhubilaiPortrait.jpg_commons.wikimedia.org; p. 29 LMspencer/Shutterstock.com; p. 30 Hung Chung Chih/Shutterstock.com.

Printed in the United States of America

CPSIA compliance information: Batch #CWENS25: For further information, contact Enslow Publishing at 1-800-398-2504.

CONTENTS

Words in the glossary appear in **bold** the first time they are used in the text.

Into the Past

People have lived in modern China for hundreds of thousands of years! Around 2000 BCE, they began to form communities. The many accomplishments of ancient China—from tools to paper—began to **develop** just a few hundred years later!

LEARN MORE

Ancient means very old or having been around a long time.

MONGOLIA
Ulaanbaatar
GOBI
CHINA
Ürümqi
Hohhot
Beijing
Harbin
Changchun
Zhengzhou
Yinchuan
Yumen
Xian
Wuhan
Hotan
Chengdu
Chongqing
Guiyang
Kunming
Lhasa
Xiamen
Macau
KOREA
LAOS
THAILAND
BANGLADESH
Kolkata
Nay Pyi
INDIA
Delhi
Jabalpur
Hyderabad
BAY OF BENGAL
Chennai
Panaji
Bangalore
LANKA

THE LAND

Ancient people settled along the Huang He, or Yellow River. The river became known as the **cradle** of Chinese **civilization.** When the river spilled over its banks, it created good farmland. However, the floods also caused great ruin.

LEARN MORE

Other cradles of ancient civilizations are the Indus River in India, the Nile River in Egypt, and the Tigris and Euphrates Rivers in modern Iraq.

Yellow River

China's **geography** has made it hard to invade, or enter by force. It has huge desert areas, such as the Gobi Desert in the north. The Himalayas on China's southwest border have some of the tallest mountains in the world!

Gobi Desert

LEARN MORE

Ancient Chinese civilization grew without much outside influence, or effect, for thousands of years. This is in part because of the land's geography.

Himalayas

What Is a Dynasty?

Historians often break down ancient Chinese history by the ruling dynasty. A dynasty is a line of rulers who belong to a single family. Some ruling families believed in the mandate of heaven. This was the idea that heaven gave an emperor, or ruler, the right to govern.

LEARN MORE

Some people think the Xia dynasty was the first to rule China, but historians know little about this time. The dynasty may have begun to gain power around 2100 BCE.

Yu the Great,
Xia dynasty

The Shang dynasty was the first to leave written records and **artifacts.** It ruled from about 1600 BCE to 1046 BCE. The people who lived under the Shang dynasty used a metal called bronze to make weapons, or arms; tools; and **religious** objects.

bronze knives, Shang dynasty

LEARN MORE

Historians have found bones and shells with early Chinese writing on them from the Shang dynasty. These artifacts have told them a lot about the time period.

water bowl,
Shang dynasty

The Time of the Zhou

The Zhou overthrew the Shang dynasty in 1046 BCE and ruled until 256 BCE. During this time, people began to better control the Chinese rivers. It made farming easier. The people of the Zhou dynasty invented money and a writing system, among other accomplishments.

LEARN MORE

Many important people lived during the Zhou dynasty, such as the great **philosopher** Confucius!

plate with ancient writing, Zhou dynasty

Confucianism and Taoism both began during the Zhou dynasty. These two philosophies helped create the Chinese **culture** that's still around today. Confucianism teaches the importance of **responsibility** and kindness. Taoism teaches its followers to live a simple life of good works.

LEARN MORE

Buddhism, Confucianism, and Taoism are called the "three teachings" or "three ways" because they're the most important philosophies in Chinese culture.

热烈庆祝中华人民共和国成立70周年

From Qin to Han

After a period without a main dynasty, the Qin dynasty began in 221 BCE. It didn't last long, but this dynasty began connecting, or joining, walls built around the empire. These walls were ancient parts of what's now called the Great Wall of China.

LEARN MORE

Qin, which sounds like "chin," is believed to be where the modern name "China" comes from.

Great Wall of China

The Han dynasty rose to power in 206 BCE. It set up a strong government. Paper was invented during the Han dynasty! However, the dynasty fell around 220 CE. China didn't have just a single ruler for more than 350 years after that.

ancient coins, Song dynasty

LEARN MORE

Rule by the Sui, Tang, and Song dynasties—which lasted from about 581 to 1279 CE—had advances in science and art.

rock **carvings**,
9th–13th century CE

The Silk Road

Areas of China traded goods outside of Asia before 200 BCE. But the trade of goods, such as a soft, shiny cloth called silk, began to happen even more during the Han dynasty. Traders highly valued salt, paper, and tea along the Silk Road.

LEARN MORE

The Silk Road is the name used for the trade routes, or paths, that ran between modern-day Europe and China.

silk, Han dynasty

People in Western countries wanted Chinese goods, including goods made of a hard white clay called porcelain. In return, the Chinese bought cotton, gold, and glass. People also shared languages and ideas about science, philosophy, and religion along the Silk Road.

book, 250 CE, Han dynasty

LEARN MORE

Many items that are common today were invented in ancient China. The Chinese were printing books hundreds of years before Europeans!

painted pot,
Han dynasty

Mongol Takeover

The Mongolian leader Kublai Khan took over China in the 1200s. However, Chinese culture changed very little. In fact, when Kublai Khan ruled, he took on the position of Chinese emperor and even created a new dynasty called the Yuan dynasty.

LEARN MORE

The Mongols' empire connected Asian and Middle Eastern civilizations. It led to the spread of ideas and goods between China and Western countries.

Kublai Khan

The Last Dynasties

Leaders of the Ming dynasty overthrew the Mongols in 1368. In 1644, the Qing dynasty began. It lasted until 1912—the last Chinese dynasty. There's no question that ancient history shaped the Chinese culture of today!

LEARN MORE

Today, more than 1.4 billion people live in China!

present-day Shanghai, China

Timeline of Major Chinese Dynasties

c. 1600–1046 BCE .... Shang dynasty
1046–256 BCE .... Zhou dynasty
221–206 BCE.................... Qin dynasty
206 BCE–220 CE.............. Han dynasty
581–618 CE .... Sui dynasty
618–907 CE .... Tang dynasty
960–1279 CE.................... Song dynasty
1279–1368 CE... Yuan dynasty (Mongols)
1368–1644 CE .... Ming dynasty
1644–1912 CE .... Qing dynasty

GLOSSARY

artifact: Something made by humans in the past.

Buddhism: A religion that began in Asia teaching that one will suffer in life, but great focus and learning can help free a person from it.

carving: Art made by cutting into the surface of something, such as rock.

civilization: Organized society with written records and laws.

cradle: The place where something begins.

culture: The beliefs and ways of life of a group of people.

develop: To grow and change over time.

geography: The features of land such as plains or mountains.

philosopher: Someone who studies philosophy, which is a system of thought made to try to understand the nature of that which is real.

religious: Having to do with religion, or faith.

responsibility: Something one does because it is their job or because it is right to do so.

FOR MORE INFORMATION

BOOKS

Faust, Daniel R. *The Rise and Fall of Ancient China*. Minneapolis, MN: Bearport Publishing, 2025.

Hudak, Heather C. *Focus on China*. St. Catharines, Ontario, Canada: Crabtree Publishing, 2025.

WEBSITE

National Geographic Kids: China
https://kids.nationalgeographic.com/geography/countries/article/china
Find out more about China's history, geography, and more.

Publisher's note to educators and parents: Our editors have carefully reviewed this website to ensure it is suitable for students. Many websites change frequently, however, and we cannot guarantee that a site's future contents will continue to meet our high standards of quality and educational value. Be advised that students should be closely supervised whenever they access the internet.

INDEX